MEDIEVAL

MEDIEVAL

STEVEN FARMER

KRUPSKAYA • 1999

Cover Photograph by Steven Farmer
Cover Design by Thomas Bossert and Frank Mueller
Typesetting by Jocelyn Saidenberg

Some of this work appeared previously in the following publications: *Avec, Crayon, Dark Ages Clasp the Daisy Root, Lyric &, Object, Mirage#4/ Period(ical) #4, Pessimistic Labor* and *Tripwire*; as well as in the collections *"I am a Child:" Poetry after Bruce Andrews and Robert Duncan* (Tailspin Press) and *The Poetry Calendar* (Sun & Moon Press). Many thanks to the editors.

Medieval cites the following sources, indicated in the text by either altered fonts or quotation marks:
p. 12, Robert Duncan, quoting Pindar
p. 77, Karl Marx, from *Capital*
p. 90, Freedy Johnston, line from song "This Perfect World"
p. 103, Mike Amnasan in conversation, around 1995
p. 113, Joel Kuzai, NYU Poets Talk "Form" panel, 1996

for Kim, Adam, Silas & Evie

Distibuted by Small Press Distribution, Berkeley
800-869-7553
orders@spdbooks.org

ISBN 1-928650-00-7

KRUPSKAYA
PO Box 420249
San Francisco, CA
94142-0249
jocelyns@sirius.com

Contents

ONCE

hills of smoke

logarithm

the cold rocks

cellophane creek

the birds have forgotten, muzzle heat
the poor blend in. . . .   song of a truck

    standing bison, floral caverns
do not go. . . . just a guy.

Once there was a son / mosaic simpleton
design's base   (murder the better qualities)

sonar

Dept. of English & Broken
Scimitars

phoenix before a taxidermist

control frightening cloth

THIS FARM PROTECTED

Railcars steam through the withering dominance, signal a kind of attachment to fate. Like love in a tunnel, the use of the mind, the brittle canvas and pathways. The superintendent, his assistant, and other employees go unarmed at all times. Silo bins at the exposition. A radio in a swamp.

STARDUST PARASITE

Promise, promise, caterwaul
hypno-sparkler
cinema's loss

routine channel stuck (struck)
can't get away to go there

beguilement worn to dependency
flares forever momentary
(need sutured, kept from a pox
I'm so / you're so. . . .   need's a badge)

clammer and diversity of the host
(station messages)   "luck is a blot"
"the poor are spoiled"   Liars make more money

look up syrupy fortunes. . . . Heartbreak Cartel
principles stand up behind you

look up: antique reticence, glue in the jackpot
broken collected intervals. . . .

this distance, an archly rented service
lens to pretensions of big-time

spray bottles of germicidal
and disinfectant are being used on the lawn

FLAME

going up to the black, on point

"remove what I am in habit"

rectangle drain yard, hose for the mats, which Friday

city, professional flashlight brigade. . . .

envelope missing for introduction

introduction to drag and click

practice known to consume practitioners

practice with neck, spine, moral code

. . . . newer fumes for anti-mobilization
icon / idol glow. Register here

for low-risk abstraction, credibility based in ash

trope, a way to back out

"but I'm living here"   hammock, moderate cost

hacking into the storm foundation's data banks
wintering   isn't the pilot working

isn't the background flickering
luminous   not by technique alone

some intensity / transformation ratio

only for conversation or real

which time would be more convenient for you

My theory of madness

My theory of indulgence

STELLAR ANOMALY

the brightness begins its delirious
crest. The evidence stops where the brightness begins

shabby chairs brought into order

a fairground, pinwheels, a technical day

The configuration has changed its pattern
to represent desperate pageantry:

original marbled edges of hunger, given to expectation

it has held its position over the hill
by the barn, the gas and the calendar

it has held its position, put flags around something fried
go home where the ceiling is fixed

he sewed the ribbon she wore in
her hair to his chest until it bled

our identities and the products we use
return with the weekend dynamic

B HOOD

conscience woke up to severe limitations

the best of intentions, amended

separate exits / frequent catharsis

how to get close in film

the part where years are fully lengthened

credit, more of available now

to election, a toast archaic, pop-up contour

the ardor of refunds in Normal Heights

list ghosts, no other guests for casting

rakes are innocent, own it, desire

city patient for make-overs / unsure whether to wave

a fry cook senses prosecution

a row of dark hats at the DA's office

intimate isn't it / enter Madame

the delicacies we already know

meticulously crafted for contemporary tastes

continuing prosperity of the west

sorrow of numbers hangs transfixed

a diligent legion to pour the syrup

alarm every letter to random

MAN IN THE GUTTER

ugh stasis
sentinel's horns
the great past
collection motor

dark moon / feed attack
a joke about fighting
a death in the projects

fist
rain railroad road
extinct tool & dye
charm electro-mechanical sensate
hum

slump
fits of the sky in vain
some sun among haze
in the song box / civic

chromatic entrance
strigae return chromatic
circle the black ring

ruin guitar & cannister
warehouse
bust in the rain. . . . *ceramica*

DISASSEMBLE

materials known to the state
to cause a suspension of disbelief

tepid requiem
safety in anonymity

factory / forest / office, alert

for breakfast, a trucker's lunch
is the highlight (mention collapse, get half off)

trellis of summer and nimrod cups
the curfew's been lifted to whenever you can make it

noir or muffle the noir

inexpensively disconcerted easy living, the distribution
of some kind of beetle or small chocolate

drop the fingerprint records, credit reports
distinguishing marks or scars on the body

harmonious purchasing, strong language, nudity, violence
rise to the top, compete

next, a remarkable family visits
cultural peasantry

now as else

lottery mocking the state's sobriety, odorless and loud

THE BEGINNING OF SIGHT

for Diane Ward

black eye promising
aperture open to change

Attendance is Feeling

tube of acrylic with flight to a local address

Strap-on Bandoleers

a not so sunset, wrenched from the barely visible
. . . shows up warm?

irony speaks from a place
of false protection and motion sensors

study the lighting, some hills and a freeway

any questions addressing form
are allowed in order of their submission

Primer for fever, paint the town Landlord White

picking the freshest looks
books, cooks, kitchens, best-selling dishes and more

they're the metaphor doctorates, decorate
smarter trouble you might be headed for

destination: a bleaching effect
on the landscape
match at the end of the tunnel

expectations of disaster or hope
a self-fulfilling prophecy theme park

nations prepare for (wallpaper) war

everything had been cleared from the beaches
from syringes to furniture

REPOSE PARAPHRASE

decorated or torn down space
where things come out eventually

something made of paper or iron, something in your hair

heart shaped cards to hold
up, money flowing for two weeks

a tacit collection of persons in the approximate earning range

aspirations that dress accordingly

marketing looks that appear to have
been forever their own aspirations

foam shapes, dream carts (air flow environments)

a typically warm summer flashed on
television screens across the country

twilight organ performance ordinance. Striking workers
scheduled to face each other some day

trained tones, favorite chains

favorite closer picture, warmer sand
against your face or mine

. . . . put to rest, inheritors. Owners tracking developments,
grateful to makers of silent things. . . .

temporary nestings. Trust in someone

pond tyranny, repose paraphrase

TAP

how can I have clapped

TERMS OF SUPPRESSION

Decor of restraint. Territorial threat of
the margin pressing a cistern, cavity, maw.

The deliberate exclusion of a desire
from consciousness, surface to depth. A catered

agreement offered to brace and embroider
the core against hell and bacteria.
Scrawl like the others did, get in, out of
here. Dream men falling into a well

who become our suppliers of lint. Dejected
beside a formal machine for wrecked
invisibility, Quixoticism addressing an

underground treasure a rogue become harmless
submits to. Intently watching the walls
to it crack. Internalization of tesserae roots.
I saw the circles under your eyes. Why

aren't there any more shrubs out here yet?
Random power source. Random lines.
Claws and honey tones living among
the angelic choir of the carnivores.

A plea for combustion, the reeds are aglow.
Their border covenant, thin and in shreds.
Formal dare of the overused moon
where beauty seems forced when the name

for it flickers, eyes bright with liquor before
they go dull, twelve beats of expression in change
at the moment of composition. Waning loyal
to give this character (pain?) Idiot carousel

spins in the lights, your money is just like mine
prompting a target's blatant caricature
. . . over-run hamlet. . . . neon food chains
some light bled to rejuvenate chronicles
some light bronzed as a voice in the blaze.

With the thought that with it we would be
armed. But how it clamps to put it on. Worn

as protection and broken by sense
on the next episode of fetters and keys.

Increasing the sheer emotion spent
embellishment a lustrous yoke
the debt incurred to get to this point
where no one would notice the debt incurred.

Where often I am not permitted
since the farms have been mechanized
at a lower volume of transformation.

"Consistent but not irresponsible desertions."

Dormant leaf. Carafe for Monsieur.

The housing calls for intransigence
as drugs have ravaged the drugs

leaving a flare on a field of incognizant thriving
asked to carry on. Where the summoned
was held as a frame, turned off. Where the critical
element left the party with nothing
to eat, and might be withheld.

Disembodied the young shoots look heavenward
which is a language of promise and vapor.

A trust in rapture and transport.
What is the desperation under that.

Freelance design and production. It broke.
Laotians are stealing the weeds.
With a great mis-trust of intellect, take
heart where it's not but its red flag is.

How many inches from trailer park pride.

How many scotches in region nine

where bells go in the sauce to give the
appetite its anonymous service
anonymous terms. To feed it.

EYE TO AUTUMN

town, a cold vantage
surprised by the heat

Narcotics is one
zoning board, theater another

evocative decomp
storefront treadmill
ideas touch all apparel, hours

advocate storms in Sonora,
Turlock, Oakdale

although nothing, submit to
one for invasion, two to come clean

likes overboard, our likes
like's disturbances

. . . . Thousand Island, aisle to the forest
find something you like

facsimile / rose

the last words left to coloring
turn it, hits go back months

UNTITLED *(carousel melody)*

melodeon, candy, a gear to the right

fantasy payback. . . rentals

clown for parking, animal shadows get longer

random celebrity, trenchant
surrender in increments

sphere of consumption, counting

immanent fringes & stoic cataracts
make her more. . . she possibly

funny lapel, a coastline

scrubbing the rocks. Locked in

"touched by a series"

a ring (the ride of her life) around
the ring you never see

we must become the people
we were when we met

for some their own small piece of heaven

for some the life of this song

for some to borrow
by pining, the lips go black

"hello from the oxygen tent"

. . . . *entanglement, insight into*

McPlasto

future, fossil

STROBE

anathema to explanation

mud denies the electrics

audit sweep / low light

border stopped the inventory

we're down (knob at off)

paintless cane / painless avenues

lulled permeating experiences, disfigured as economic

fighting potential look-alikes

a jack-in-the-box, a buzzer and a doll

non-drowsy relief

the critical lost (distraction) incantations from a leather mouth

demonstration of method off

ashes spread on the shoulders and back

a voice told him to stop painting

the hired help is under the lake (Dolores wake up)

beginning of debt

Versace crunch (Fifi's belt)

inside this elegant party atmosphere

apt. east, west apt.

appearance is every opportunity

journalist in a tavern

off the coast, a fleet of tankers (home)

reflective of what doesn't

intuitive leap (stable sands)

shaken utopic, decade

poverty of (up for) progress (grabs)

unified by subtraction

the dignity of a captured town

perimeter to blackout

MAN IN A DREAM

thematic space for participant fear

fog set
an ensemble of lights

"writing into a tomb"

navigators are
prone on this vessel

one more captain. . . . a make-up man

wall: trenches the thrushes might burst from

wall: thrushes that threaten to burst

patois romantique
(patois of
if anything, drone at the corner)

lack of accretion patterns to be complete
(a love-struck analyst's socks)

dripping clocks
work in suspect employ

"Sunny today in the San Fernando. . ."

approach stained with theory, a slow patrol

the course and rustic
(coupled with the serene) hours are false

hours, no inks, dyes or perfumes
commissioned by art
watch the lips and face of someone

feel the story's resonance

(symbolism does not apply)

laughter for mascots (hold them down)
intrinsic worth . . . . aggressive frost. . . .

ideas enter a marketplace
(figs fall black in the lengthening shadows)

are you going to hit those numbers
(razorback clams go down like velvet)

In the next century one company will. . . .

substance as disappearance (flares)
tiny uniform handwriting

SATED FABLES

detach at that or any

directions to multiplex, all needs met

CA to re-invent yourself

food hut coastline / the passive for "cod"

contrarier   AM Gold of the Seventies

places you, come home to tune them out

for all years

where years allowed, dwellings sit

no longer cover or natural

1933 DUST

production's squall on a roadmap
acres Juned, property's mission of theft
spores in a ballad of afterthoughts
conservation the stacking of crates in the heat
should these injuries prove redemptive
puppet theater, anger managed/
mined, perform these tasks and duties
aged in French & American plywood
father, lacking takes on its sensational airs
tickets litter the floor of the grandstand
addressing the dead, an appropriation
crop of the necro, indentured

MEDIEVAL

Cloak the blueprint of hills

color the likeness

versus royalty

comic will hurt

entendre

life in a panel

back up human & animal

minus. . . . and all that begins with a minus

how I pray

barbiturate

history

work site. . . . will you go away

golem

oven room

rune emission

circuit timed to fire trees

silver berry

punitive jolt

rigged arm of attentive staff

the pulling, remote

near description of caste

knocking. . . . broken. . . . given

usable petrification

circuit

wind of Crom

conquest capitol

grey sky cloud grid

silencer tympanum

sound won't be mentioned

district abstract

calls up individual memories

recognition verdigrised

stray light

base unhinged

brass children turn away

dried plant appetizer

happier homes are pictured

personal sand

personal anecdote

boulevard vacant

a port

a highway a name

remarkable shelf life

an edict of stars, what brain speed

collapse in a blaze of success

broken glare

the *Rue de Sandwiche*

no respect due these phantoms

transients switched to forward

relay, toggle switch

fiction & affidavit

throttled melody

foundry cast

computer tracks a path to the garret

single distorted figure's jealousy

income taken serious

we'll feed at the back

sentry arrives with paychecks

misfortune smiles a history

creased and denied

exhaust hood & sky crack

cloud at land's underbelly. . . . fish

mold or wreath of black gelatin tonight

flag light is out of a tower

dunce of speech to escape

corrosion rogue

proletarian cake

invited to rule

frozen lease

misinformed trimming

job of the ambler

holiday bird is a plant

prevalent Average Merchant Fever Day

they're not paying me

I'm not showing up

farm in a matrix

there isn't a ritual

death is for shivering medical file

young buyers will not be young

Kensington daughter stockpile

rustic

I have one

the envelope please. . . . somehow

award the region its missing

when she's near the farmwork patches shadow

modulate

loomer sepia

plates disengage

wir forest

Emily threads her back to a lathe

ice tree crystalline

shaken crest

no longer people

ethereal lattice

reference somehow realm of the comic

signal eyes comb thermal backlight

awash, rogue of greater sins   list abdication, know them

intruder, their world is more complete than ours

they walk around like creeps

tangible town / yellow lights

aspire ownership

tangible town

by-products poison the storyboards

toxic wards of the state, sleep

the bells of the courtyard rang for mackerel

put on your game face

this week's shifts

imagined romance of occupation

commensurate with experience

pay commensurate with class

let ring soften to flavor

the romance of isolation

on your own, targets are flowers

protector was hit, press any key to return

permanent light sought in forms

feel better knocked out

self-predator having distanced

measure my craft by how I have distanced

sheer numbers free to damage

great shadow is not to leave

vowel trench

obeyer curse

white poison had taken

. . . . white poison had taken the legend. . . . yellow land
& unripe fruit have promise / bad things are fuel

participants are reluctant
in the description of the field

participants are reluctant
in the description of the field

compliant and basic visual concepts
of altar intimidation and zeal

participants are reluctant
in the description of the field

loss forest

station of timing

re-colonization

disorder / authority

fiend or servant to do my bidding

bound and not repentant

'affirmative will'

interpreted workers

recently annexed exhuberance

errors, the painting surrounded

his fifty hours, a physical stencil

affirmative, floral, etched in recovery

waking to work. . . . as the babies get older they

bump their heads, start to see different

alarm clocks, condoms

protected avarice

musical pimp. . . . tome of shards

supplication

cloaking device

cold of the winter

blade occupation

white folds a red brown blood on

the snow. . . . tent arrested

clay on her neck and thighs

the obedient animal saddest of all

no public assemblage of three

manufactured assemblage

posture confusion

thunderous blades of digital shading

wreck by wreck the technology spread

retention of information winter

rote absorption of moods

reflection thaw hard coal of masculine

brutal palace

commiseration of lambs

portrait confusion

a tree of light

by fear to tend

shield, a given pact

upheld   for burning

brace the dark / unseed

a beckoned prop, demise

bedding of tinder

"may we enter"

"may we return"

the sentinel

gang mythos empowering youth

the guard

fruition of penance

truck month

violet lamb. . . . in the night the white of

a planet behind a mule

leather tunic's shudder

rote

cul de sac

neighbors can't

patrons say they'd like to see

hermetic, & its irritant

great senior citizen complex

line-up of the planets, means

red and green in the gold mud

candle pentagram in the mud

unearthed lot. . . . tangle of wires

FASHION   FATE   PLAZA

domination to free the

secular blanket, housing clouds

        the uniforms are a big part of it

patch returning, job's resolve

everything in the past is brown

I don't know what kind of an
angel would fall asleep in his food dish

mist in the valley, nouveau riche
family epoch having been broken

backward ascension, the rain of trash
intelligence leading to cynicism

an effortless grace in the way it
connects the killing events to an order

cognition stripped them of innocence

a vengeance to be similar

crow broke, insane

over the slanted mountain, fear

the guitars sound like cans

physics bitch, dark cables of hair

purchase stuck in orthodoxy
mirrors, stains, bottles of ink

enormous bags (dried faces)
mall of the valley, aflame in trade

the comforting nature of
washed out things before the margins close. . . .

fine art pantomime

wheelbarrow contestants

decorated in anonymity, sentimental design flaws

enormous nights / ancient can interpreter
beautifully typewritten exegesis trance (this is his city)
of flats & heights, observation planes of astonishing impersonality

residue   pall   distrust

mute star is a crown among branches
the wind blew in to defeat the flame

the carnivore in the plan
who seemed a better drunk for my lord

detergent   ingredients   plastic

who must be fed

simmer and plagiarist farce

the immobile blocks when we feel like little

carpenters-- like you to live

to consume-- a lot

and your body is just like a factory   temple

come up with energy   take away thought

a vote for configurations of taste

if mold develops, unwind

the syllables live in a sleeve

dock past adversity, season the plate not

porno?   meat dry-aged in a sermon, asunder

to take it out of

harm's way   a gash in a tablet

relieves these walls of their thunder

they back up in two-dimensional slabs

decamero'clock with a deviant

caddies for low-cost history

accurate practices, polyurethane storage

for elders, not to have seen in time

"revolution" a university class

in chartreuse or navy

better for chapters

cliffs hang over the dark pulp

compliance, intangibles having more broth

with a history, fees go to sea bells

sea bells knick

fledgling emitted a rasp

apparition museum

May 4 - June 23

appliances, twigs for phone poles

descriptive adjectives

now you can't get out

the upper of several units

so much of this life is imagined

up with several

parking appeared in the work

the only thing that will help a sour mouth

apparition, script for the mute

the pack fed on its members. Haunted by a memory of trust

another court of thick defense
    because division cleanses

Cartel aware

it must live in bronze

to be placid, falsely

demotic   given the right interior

feeling of locking

"circumferent juniper "   "kerosene grass"

in a trench awaiting the sun's approach

in the cautious pastoral fraught

missive

mattresses, goats

magnificent grounds

hams broken with great gentility

blacken the flaking of words

to butter a richness   chaos   a lark

In a block long plot of land across the street from where I was born What is a working day? were ruined foundations, the shells of old cement Navy housing without roofs What is the length of time among mustard seed and wild sagebrush during which capital may consume weeds where as a child I would fantasize seeing a disheveled, sandy-haired drifter of high character, part Harry O, part Joe South, the labor power whose daily value it buys virtuous, honest, but sort of... punished It has been said that to these questions capital replies: persecuted or at the very least "misunderstood" The working day contains the full twenty-four hours an outcast who held no station but was the immediate friend of children and the elderly; it is self evident that the laborer should have had a dog but didn't, is nothing else, his whole life through, than labor power, was like a dog himself in some ways, that therefore all his disposable time is by nature and law labor time spent meaningless time with you, joked, a quiet smile, to be devoted had beach sand in a Mexican knapsack he carried, to the expansion of capital was as much there as not. Older siblings would fulfill this role were they not Time for education, for intellectual development, for the fulfilling of social functions tied to the family romance and could be outside, for social intercourse, for the free play of his bodily and mental activity, a projection of their potential --sunshine! shortening the extent of the laborer's life I see sea-foam green as a greedy farmer snatches increased produce from the soil and dunes brushed by the salt ocean air, robbing it of its fertility, my favorite colors

saturate plurality in all its incompletion

sleep demands where the money is

a coveted intellect sets its borders for fabricated meaning

the fabric of currency must be neutral in order to represent value cloth on the rock

sky / invented dieties

marvel at and contain the irregular

clearest belonging

obscured and interrupted

place between magic and clutter

"I always feel like"

civilization is recent

carvings absolve the responsible

blood. . . . darkness. . . . laughter an axe

aspiration to fill the lack

popularity reaches uselessness

cooling trend

comparison of scars

old men listen to Ozzy

cello bring the age to light

obliterate the dulcimer

a beat held the moss in place

fold to mark the startled walls

sketch our spindled frame there

metrically inaccurate

tear back in cruelty

the mask and its effect

canyon spit its name back

slanted and of known rocks

no rocks from these environs

these are unidentified flying rocks

how can I be of service to you

through service eradicate my faults

the sound of bells has been calling for years

preposterous to be human

skein of toppling sounds

spent, the mounting of a stump

green dank of onerati

casts its interference

what authority it holds

to crank it down, crank's battened

an alive gear to call-- of faith

no other rage is possible

(barco pirata

(hombre fuerte

I heard your broadcast last night
the throes of trucks on the interstate
I thought the colors warded off
the simple man we think of
ten dividers for the seven teams
embrace the limitations
a geography that cancels
when he comes back even larger
larger ounces in all the cups
good with tools. . . . moving unflustered
among the trees and crosses

aisle of the splintered standards

& *enormous nights,* hoods, markets

gearing up for a scan of tarts   (canon at the trough)

years of austerity conquered

property ownership values

design values, argued research

hygenic formica surfaces

his life of toil, isolate leisure

provided for a time what's important

loaded, can't return

ridalin nomadic

the outsiders speed across the country in a car

meaningless cinematic releases link the disparate communities

nailing the bread to the shelves

a seam in the earth

approaches to visualization

footnotes can't get radiant

by consent, cobbled steps in

resemblance of resting

I think that was magic

more stocks for peasanthood

soil and ambient

moonlit, what they brought to the table

telephony, socks from a tree

in a blanket, apartment display box

reaching the plug, invisible

12 at night

gaze from under a cloak   *(la dompna)*

calm and feral eyes

in the apartment later

the apartment is open

if you are unable to work

if you have passed away and can't work

// the password to this log is
a correction with a red hand

// the password to this log is
seven lines cut the thicket

// the password to this log is
the margins taunt & harry

// the password to this log is
unlicensed in its comment

// the password to this log is
locks in dark sound tumble

// the password to this log is
indulgent & intoned

// the password to this log is
by the hound of a past form

// the password to this log is
"lock this after me"

parent narrative go away

clouds and vertical bars

grid a foam landscape in chrome for a surge

stare at medical terms that erase

the root system's network aluminum

every sector a blank in the desert of lights

sod of black metal & night-blooming jasmine

corked, Arnaut Daniel in the distance

doesn't it won't go forth (use supersoil

baffler) vintage suprised by time

when I went back the village was smaller

did somebody die for you to wear

so much mauve   the wage of a famous man stacking

toil of mistakes in the pepper grenache

National Anti-Depressant Clause

imagines an era of stress and blame

complicit monolith

cubicle want

shoelace endorsement

fix it

masking you, imitate bird songs

or gunfire, canso of dry & bare scrub-rock

thyme and flat lavender *orange cheese*

is the only cheese we know

and sad was happy there uttering

patron company's artists

concoct the next visual on the screen

as each of these small deletions will add to the resumé a particular sheen

tuck in, shave
get milk for polis
ride on the back of strife
tired replays axed

myth in a culvert, lights
out to please you
become so afraid for
living to benefit

night charade ruinous   anyone's

leathering

mask on a dome   wither

countenance   any

adapted background, a coat of wheat
service life of abundance

separate, common, encrypted, a thing of evil
had to be written in bad tights

blowhards lean by the barrels
living in cloth like costed units

decreasing, muse of the weathervane
shadow the yard

sfumato Caprese / nostalgia's immediate
none of us can critique art

the populism of Nashville

the exchange of tortured madrigals

hello sugar tongue

sound displaced the meaning

honeyed form became the critical

eradication cycle

we begin-- are you infected

what is seen

black significance

sing, play the spinnet

template's order song

erase

to atone & leave dormant

a collection of pens

by the fire where my swollen hand

violence commission

the creation of a portrait

wherein toxins are stored

rule of decadence & cinema

finds dour honorary

fiends in the literature

enter the sordid kitchen

flowered promise of the Medici

legacy of the odors

we're taken very seriously

some fear the passage of time

that was the year that I got tough

enter the slow-witted vampire

town of the culinary oaf

'feudal world of important thinkers'

proper documentation

broken lair, missing tickets

they cannot be identified

a value given to the mental

methods no more ruthless than

the opposition's offering

padded light

identity

a seeking malady housed

enter the blank competitor

area of the black chart

called in from the brake of reeds

internalize the structure

so the work culture isn't false

masters of appearances

smoke and mirrors

trap continuation of the imprint

each faded cast

each performance from the clam shell

a present crutch requiring

dispute resolution

a jagged path, blame lit

across the seven counties

an inversion of the stars at night

the name of one thing for another

dark tome's sleeve locked

black shells hang in space

future such an *information*   *you've escaped*

avenge the children's weathering

compass the besotted bay

tide to plot a crime by

art on hold

return the tongs

impractical

"we get along"

any month, oblation

close / personal

of white-out

strengthen opposite muscle groups

a mental picture filed away

dandelion greens to the south

sauce doesn't go in boats anymore

afterglow as ambush

urgent capital far away

strength / wax   remove the covenant

wires frayed on the underside

sponsored by the invisible body   (reconciliation to it)

where inabilities trigger pride
the implicit throng's opinions shift
a dull cognition's dollar of honor
the last breath of a popular form
a thing of beauty commisioned trash
the way a forest guards its rot
inseminating a number of frauds
the heart's tricks are reserved for dragging
        bodily fluids had ruined the cloth

by an ochre sauce that put them to sleep

dark astronomy where the ingredients marry
every note in a loom of heat

subjectivity grouped in

the quiet production

hard light / soft light patio

headaches of comfort

belonging, agreement of wares

analyses of those found asleep

in redemption

neighbor persona and stature

assistance needed to conjure

diploma, exchange is two percent

of this chicken / check every channel

seduction, oxen *tomato paste in my fettucine*

farm-torn herbs on my pizza / pizzetta

a transposition of separate elements palm trees

tortoises, fuschia & friars watch this packaging make its

claims to the loon of night & in marble

far from the fear of originals

bristling

my name is Sergio and I am destined for economic ruin

loss of beguilement syndrome

loss of melody syndrome

loss of personification syndrome

loss of personnel syndrome

loss of directive to formulate syndrome

loss of intimacy syndrome or LOIS

loss of remedial skill distinction syndrome

loss of navigational correlative syndrome

loss of proportionate effort syndrome (LOPES)

loss of evident mirth syndrome (LOEMS)

enter the blank competitor

housed in sevens where the fairies lived

a false magic protects a dial frozen in the yard

haggard verse, the week gave way to

"the appearance of an insight"

reinforced the larger, separate

discreet use of form

technically, somnambulists

the bright shaft of learning

trained, ornaments are bogged

cloud's napped, could be molded blue

molded white to fend

heaven's practice of opacity, portension

of a central link an amulet would promise to a bead

wont' let him in unless he is a Padre or an A

stadium of tall hats

song of Harlem sauntering

big mood and feedback

Ellington

symphonic

gumball has a dedication

evocateur of larger cranes

scored where the pier drops

solvent to a greater force

beige dream of rent

froth, pigeon coop romantics

quality assembly

"trust this absence of a feedback"

think in lines, kill the skeptic sleep

a week's compression read

glazed seven forms of ruse

jewel box in monochrome

sound world in ink

Glitter Gulch

The Four Queens

Cypress

Aqua

Ginger Glitch

Roman Holiday

Citron

Stella

Maitre d' Mattress

Black Soup

Bojo's Shed

Idea Fish

The Torn Shiitake

Cinder Box

Scarves are Us

Without A Name

We Tie It Up

A Toque of Fright

~~Burger Dirge~~

~~The Dark Frappe~~

a poetics of exhaustion

hello team player

a fierce attraction, peppered

and the merchants cling, apend

children have no parents   the apt.
soothing   heaped

busy cultured demiurge
so now is then belied

*   *   *

prayer haunted   shape of
felt where certain   hated
texture flowers

troubled surface   foil for moods
before the drop to darken it

employment feigned identity

his second nature jacket

small light   to see and canvas

tunnel   barred   careen

*   *   *

inflicted benefactor

claim the wind that brushed the canvas

at stake a replication

slashing strokes devoid of testament

walnut panel

in the hill   succumb again

to walls

absent patrons dry the passion

made coherent   cope

*   *   *

to soothe the sleep

lose what won't be dreamt

the book's metonymy

low impact / input

eerie realist security

safety in the subject

matter, block contamination

monody *in vacuo*

balance   isolation

*   *   *

contextual   the rendered

foreign precipice

surrendered cake

elation? disavowed

a chance confirmed the contact

heretic

wand will bring the moondust

comfort, masked remaining dialect

attention captured, trivia

bereft   intoxin cola

*   *   *

by restitution   storm the link   come alive

bereft   clod at luminator's

911 to beg the right address

going onto one knee with a spoon
from one generation to the next
going onto one knee with a spoon
for nothing to be left vulnerable

going onto one knee with a spoon
taking orders from ceremony
going onto one knee with a spoon
the loss of his mother's smile

going onto one knee with a string
bread sculpted into a cluster of grapes
going onto one knee with a string
ladles for cheese-making hang in the caseificio

from one generation to the next
going onto one knee with a spoon
furniture fabric depicting the farmworker's struggle
going onto one knee with a spoon

the people will neither read nor write
going onto one knee with a spoon
inheriting seemingly ghost-like qualities
going onto one knee with a spoon

going onto one knee by sedition
the troubled boy is a laughing stock
a world lit only by fire
the destruction of letters by fire

going onto one knee by sedition
picking through ruins was drying their hands out
going onto one knee by sedition
to recognize the investment

going onto one knee by sedition
going onto one knee with a spoon
developing a unique bond with a wolf
salted wounds

going onto one knee with a spoon
flageolets, crumbling mirepoix
going onto one knee with a spoon
gaze of the underwhelmed